Marriage Is a Promise of Love

A Blue Mountain Arts® Collection
About the Most Beautiful Commitment
Two Hearts Can Share

Special Updated Edition

Edited by Gary Morris

Blue Mountain Press®
Boulder, Colorado

Library of Congress Control Number: 2003110230
ISBN: 978-0-88396-759-1

ACKNOWLEDGMENTS appear on page 64.

Certain trademarks are used under license.
BLUE MOUNTAIN PRESS is registered in U.S. Patent and Trademark Office.

Printed in the United States of America.
Fifth Printing: 2007

 This book is printed on recycled paper.

This book is printed on fine quality, laid embossed, 80 lb. paper. This paper has been specially produced to be acid free (neutral pH) and contains no groundwood or unbleached pulp. It conforms with all the requirements of the American National Standards Institute, Inc., so as to ensure that this book will last and be enjoyed by future generations.

Blue Mountain Arts, Inc.
P.O. Box 4549, Boulder, Colorado 80306

Contents

Marriage Is...

 A commitment. Its success doesn't depend on feelings, circumstances, or moods — but on two people who are loyal to each other and the vows they took on their wedding day.

Hard work. It means chores, disagreements, misunderstandings, and times when you might not like each other very much. When you work at it together, it can be the greatest blessing in the world.

A relationship where two people must listen, compromise, and respect. It's an arrangement that requires a multitude of decisions to be made together. Listening, respecting, and compromising go a long way toward keeping peace and harmony.

A union in which two people learn from their mistakes, accept each other's faults, and willingly adjust behaviors that need to be changed. It's caring enough about each other to work through disappointing and hurtful times, and believing in the love that brought you together in the first place.

Patience and forgiveness. It's being open and honest, thoughtful and kind. Marriage means talking things out, making necessary changes, and forgiving each other. It's unconditional love at its most understanding and vulnerable — love that supports, comforts, and is determined to triumph over every challenge and adversity.

Marriage is a partnership of two unique people who bring out the very best in each other and who know that even though they are wonderful as individuals... they are even better together.

∽ Barbara Cage

The Journey of Marriage Begins with Love

Falling in love is like being
first to discover the most beautiful
    thing in the world
or find something so lovely
that no one else had ever noticed.
It's like glimpsing the first
    evening star
or the rainbow that unexpectedly
appears in the midst of a storm.

Love often starts in little ways.
It comes quietly with a smile,
    a glance, or a touch,
but you know it's there
because suddenly you're not alone
and the sadness inside you is gone.
Love means finally finding a place
    in this world
that shelters you and is your
    very own —
where you feel you have been forever
and you live and grow and learn.

                                   ~ Vickie M. Worsham

The Perfect Soul Mate Is Someone Who...

- will watch you while you sleep
- will kiss you out of a bad dream
- will love every inch of your body
- will laugh, cry, and share with you
- will celebrate with you
- will cherish every feeling
  you experience
- will be grateful that you're you
- will whisper sweet somethings
  in your ear
- will encourage you to follow
  your dreams
- will always be on your side
- will love you unconditionally

≥ Miranda Moti

Words from the Heart of a Husband and Wife

"I want to grow old with you,
lose count of the sunsets we share,
stroll along a moonlit beach —
always holding hands and looking into
each other's eyes with deep longing —
no matter our age.
I want memories of sitting by a campfire,
warm conversation filling the
crisp forest air between us,
and evening whispers among the trees
filling my soul with love for you.
I want to wake beside you each morning
and feel the brightness and warmth
of your sunshine on my face.
I want to travel the world
with you beside me,
explore the space between our souls,
and feel the ever-growing love
that feeds our spirits.
I want to feel the universe between us,
sit beneath the clear evening sky,
imagine heaven, and thank God for
the gift of you.

I want to play in the snow,
make angels, and write messages of love
with my gloved hand.
I want to face the challenge of conveying
to you this deepening love I have.
Trying to tell you how much
I love you is like translating
beautiful music into something
that is still and silent —
yet I shall always make the effort,
though it seems as impossible as
describing heaven.

I want you beside me
as my best friend and lover.
Always.
I want you forever with me,
forever soul mates,
today and always...
beyond tomorrow."

                       Tim M. Krzys

If You Want to Share the Best Kind of Love...

Value your partner's talents. Express how much you treasure the other's special gifts.

Accept the challenges that test your relationship. See each challenge not as an overwhelming problem, but as an opportunity to strengthen your love.

Listen to each other. Be there to acknowledge your partner's needs and feelings with your whole heart and soul.

Encourage your loved one to grow as an individual, and explore opportunities for your own growth. Expect each other to be the best person they can be.

Nurture your partnership. Laugh, dance, and romance each other. Share an optimistic outlook and a spirit of fun.

Tell each other "I love you." Talk about the good times you've shared and your plans to make even more joyful memories.

Inquire about your partner's day. Express interest in each other's dreams, plans, and activities.

Notice each other's positive features. Compliment generously when you like a new outfit, a new haircut, or a new anything that matters to your loved one.

Expect that your relationship will keep getting better and better. Act on that expectation and never settle for less. Give the best of your love and your friendship, and commit to a partnership built on a solid foundation of faith, trust, and total devotion to each other.

                                                 ～ Jacqueline Schiff

A Marriage Creed

Love is the strongest and
most fulfilling emotion possible
It lets you share
your goals, your desires, your experiences
It lets you share
your life with someone
It lets you be yourself
    with someone who will always support you
It lets you speak
your innermost feelings
    to someone who understands you
It lets you feel tenderness and warmth —
    a wholeness that avoids loneliness
Love lets you feel complete

But in order to have
a successful love relationship
you must make a strong commitment
    to each other and love
and you must do and feel everything
    within your mind and body
    to make this commitment work

You must be happy with yourself
    and you must understand yourself before
    you can expect someone else to be happy
    with you or to understand you
You must be honest about yourself
    and each other at all times
    and not hold any feelings back
You must accept each other the way you are
    and not try to change each other
You must be free to grow as individuals
    yet share your life as one
    but not live your life through each other
You must follow your own principles and morals
    and not follow what societal roles
    tell you to do

You must follow the philosophy that men and
　　women are equal and not treat either person
　　with inferiority in any way
You must be together always in your heart
　　but not necessarily always in your activities
You must be proud of each other and love
　　and not be ashamed to show
　　your sensitive feelings
You must treat every day
　　spent with each other as special
　　and not take each other
　　or your love for granted
You must spend time talking
　　with each other every day
　　and not be too busy with outside events
　　that you are too tired for each other
You must understand each other's moods and
　　feelings and not hurt each other intentionally
　　but if your frustrations are taken out on each other
　　you must both realize
　　that it is not a personal attack
You must be passionate with each other often
　　and not get into boring patterns
You must continue to have fun
　　and excitement with each other
　　and not be afraid to try new things
You must always work at love
　　and your love relationship
　　and not forget how important
　　this relationship is
　　or what you would feel like without it

Love is the strongest
and most fulfilling emotion possible
You will be living your dreams
　　between awakenings
if you culminate your commitment to love
with marriage

　　　　　　　　　　　　　　　　　∂ Susan Polis Schutz

A Wife Is
a Partner for Life

Life with your wife is a kind of journey through love. You have times of laughter when the sun seems to rise in your hearts and everything is perfect. You also have to hold on to each other and make it through times that challenge who you are and what you mean to each other.

You experience moments that will live forever in your minds. Your marriage can be a shining example of what two people can achieve when their hearts are in tune and their spirits are set free by trust and support to follow their dreams.

Most of all, you learn what it means to truly love — to dedicate your hearts to the commitment, sacrifice, and awareness it takes to make love last forever.

           ❧ Jon Peyton

What Is a Husband?

He is someone who realizes
    that strength of character
is more important than being tough.
He can be tender and kind,
    and he doesn't misuse his authority.
He is generous, and enjoys
    giving as well as receiving.
He is understanding;
    he tries to see both sides
        of a situation.
He is responsible;
    he knows what needs to be done,
        and he does it.
He is trustworthy;
    his word is his honor.
He loves humor, and looks
    at the bright side of things.
He takes time to think
    before he reacts.
He loves life, nature, discovery,
    excitement, and so much more.
He is a little boy sometimes,
    living in an adult body
and enjoying the best of both worlds.

                                   ⌇ Barbara Cage

Marriage Joins Two People in the Circle of Its Love

Marriage is a commitment to life — to the best that two people can find and bring out in each other. It offers opportunities for sharing and growth no other human relationship can equal, a physical and emotional joining that is promised for a lifetime.

Within the circle of its love, marriage encompasses all of life's most important relationships. A wife and husband are each other's best friend, confidant, lover, teacher, listener, and critic. There may come times when one partner is heartbroken or ailing, and the love of the other may resemble the tender caring of a parent for a child.

Marriage deepens and enriches every facet of life. Happiness is fuller; memories are fresher; commitment is stronger; even anger is felt more strongly, and passes away more quickly.

Marriage understands and forgives the mistakes life is unable to avoid. It encourages and nurtures new life, new experiences, and new ways of expressing love through the seasons of life.

When two people pledge to love and care for each other in marriage, they create a spirit unique to themselves, which binds them closer than any spoken or written words. Marriage is a promise, a potential, made in the hearts of two people who love, which takes a lifetime to fulfill.

                                               ∾ Edmund O'Neill

Secrets of a Successful Marriage

- Having a wonderful partner.
- Communicating.
- Being intimately involved in one another's life. (Open, honest, touching, together. The closer you are, the more secure you will feel.)
- Being happy as individuals. (And bringing good things to the relationship from both directions.)

- Reaching out for dreams together.
- Always being there for one another. (Always.)
- Overlooking the few flaws. (But cherishing the thousands of things that are so wonderful.)

- Remembering that rainbows follow rain.

- Always sharing. (Friends, families, dreams, desires. Weaving together the fabric of your lives.)
- And always caring. (Always loving one another, and being as happy and as giving and as thankful as any two people could be.)

∽ Chris Gallatin

Marriage Is Two People Sharing Everything in Life

In marriage
two people share
all their dreams and goals
their weaknesses and strengths
In marriage
two people share
all the joys and sadnesses of life
and all the supreme pleasures
In marriage
two people share
all of their emotions and feelings
all of their tears and laughter

Marriage is the most
fulfilling relationship
one can have
and the love that you share
as husband and wife
is beautifully forever

∾ Susan Polis Schutz

The Key to Having a Great Relationship

Always remember the wishes and the romance and all the reasons your love came to be.

Never forget that love can see you through anything; all you have to do is just let it. Never turn away from the sweetness of sharing.
You're both so incredibly lucky; never forget it.
Never let the important things go unspoken.
The dreams you have together are guideposts in your days; never forsake them. The roads you walk together will lead to a deepening joy; go hand-in-hand as best friends on your way.

Never forget that many people search all their lives for the kind of smiles you have been blessed with. Be sure to remember that love will always be life's most beautiful gift...

Share, support, speak from the heart and listen with your very souls. Know that there will be times when you may disagree; nothing could be more natural. Simply remember that when you see things from two different perspectives, you need to give and take and compromise. The longest lasting and most loving unions in the world all have moments when their journeys have uphill climbs. But the secret they share is knowing, beyond any clouds that come along, the sun will keep on shining above.

As you continue on your path together, you will come across more joys than you'll ever be able to count. And you'll keep on discovering that the "forever" kind of love is the very best thing there is.

May you <u>always</u> <u>and</u> <u>forever</u> be lovingly blessed with this exquisite and wonderful gift... because you deserve to have all the joyous rewards

   ...of a truly great relationship.

∾ Douglas Pagels

Cherish Your Anniversary

An anniversary is yesterday
cherished in the heart.
It's mountains climbed together
and new roads made.
It's believing in your dreams
and seizing the moment.
It's hearing each other's soul
and trusting in each other's choices.
It's searching for answers
and never giving up.

It's taking risks
and welcoming the adventure.
It's letting your hearts soar free
and learning from your mistakes.
It's sharing life as one,
seeing the world through
   each other's eyes,
and falling in love all over again.

∾ Linda E. Knight

Anniversaries Are for Remembering...

The day you met,
    the love you've known
The time you've shared,
    the ways you've grown

The little things that
    kept you close
The big things that
    helped you most

The joy you've felt,
    the trust you've earned
The fun you've had,
    the lessons learned

The dreams that have
    come true for you
What got you here,
    what you've been through

The promises kept,
    the commitment to stay
Together forever,
    all the way

Two special hearts
    joined as one
Two favorite people
    loved by everyone

                                      ❧ Donna Fargo

A Dozen Rules
for Couples to Live By

1. Be kind, considerate, and polite. Go out of your way to do thoughtful, nice things for each other. Say "please" and "thank you," and look for reasons to praise.

2. Be affectionate. Gentle touches, smiles, hugs, and words of endearment make your spouse feel desired and loved. Affection should be a natural, ongoing habit.

3. Be a good listener. Look at the person speaking. Listen without interrupting or becoming distracted. Be open minded, respectful, and caring.

4. Agree that it's okay to disagree. Both of you are entitled to your own feelings and beliefs. Don't judge, accuse, or insult. Look for ways to compromise and to work it out.

5. Don't berate, belittle, or nag. Each of you has a right to feel good about yourself. Don't say things that hurt, humiliate, or lower your spouse's self-esteem.

6. Be patient and understanding. Give your spouse time and space. Don't demand that things go your way. Try to see the other person's point of view.

7. Have fun. Find things you enjoy doing together and do them. Keep a sense of humor, and allow laughter to lighten your lives.

8. Help each other. Don't have "his" and "her" chores without the willingness to lend a helping hand. Make it a habit to do little things that make your spouse's life easier.

9. Forgive. No one is perfect and we all do and say things we regret. Have a forgiving heart to yourself, to others, and especially to your spouse.

10. Kiss good morning, good night, hello, and good-bye. Add a hug or a pat, and make coming together or parting special occasions that show you care.

11. Don't expect your spouse to read your mind. Be an open communicator. Let your spouse know what you want and need without being judgmental or rude.

12. Never underestimate the power of saying "I love you." Love and the acknowledgment of it keep a marriage strong and secure.

~ Barbara Cage

May Your Marriage Be Blessed with a Lifetime of Happiness

Marriage is the joining
   of two people —
the union of two hearts.
It lives on the love
   you give each other
and never grows old,
but thrives on the joy
   of each new day...
Marriage is love.

May you always be blessed
   in your hearts
with the wonder of your marriage.

May you always be able to
    talk things over,
to confide,
to laugh with each other
and enjoy life together,
to share moments
of quiet peace
when the day is done.

May you be blessed
with a lifetime of happiness.

∽ Jill Ryynanen

Let There Be No Limits to Your Love

Love is a wonderful thing. It is nourished by patience and kindness, honesty and trust, and responding gently to each other's needs. It grows by understanding and sharing feelings along the way.

Marriage is a chance for you to give and receive this love as deeply as your souls will allow.

You will become bigger and better people by listening, disagreeing, playing, crying, laughing, and forgiving.

Always love each other and believe in your individual talents and abilities... and there will be no limit to the depths of your love.

∽ Carol Howard

Marriage Is a Wonderful Journey That You Make Together

In marriage,
walk the path together,
side by side
whenever possible.
Remember to hold each other
when it is cold.
If the air becomes too close,
make a little space so each can breathe.
When the path is narrow,
pick one to go first.
Always be willing to follow;
don't be afraid to lead.
Trust your partner, trust yourself,
for marriage is a journey that
leads to great love.

❧ Mary E. Buddingh

10 Ways to Have a Happy Marriage

1. First and foremost, love each other. Realize how lucky you are to be in love with someone who loves you. Say "I love you" often and in different ways. Surprise each other often with gifts of praise. Remember that love grows in an atmosphere of freedom and trust, not from restraint and obligation. Do things to keep your love and romance new and alive. Don't take love for granted, ever. It's such a blessing.

2. Listen objectively to each other, as you would to a friend. Don't take things personally; think and react from the heart. Acceptance is a key to understanding and a buffer for tension and resentment. You don't want anyone to control your feelings, so don't try to own someone else's, not even your mate's.

3. Never stop treating each other like sweethearts. Talk to each other as sweethearts. Do things that sweethearts do. Divide up the chores around the house based on each other's preferences. Work together in achieving your goals. Do things just to make the other one feel loved, especially when he or she might be feeling a little down. Take pride in the way you look and act, not just for yourself but for your partner, but never let external values have more importance than the internal feelings of your heart.

4. Take care of each other. Go to the doctor with each other. Put the other one first, but don't neglect your own needs either. Do the things that show that you're interested in your partner's needs and desires and problems.

5. Look to each other for help. Don't let your problems or concerns get out of hand and make you go in opposite directions. Be joyful that you've each made a commitment to the other... through sickness or health, poverty or wealth, or whatever comes along. You're in this life together. Be thankful.

6. Talk about things together the way you would talk with a friend. Absolutely refuse to say anything negative about your partner. Share your most important secrets, and never betray the secrets of your partner; treat them as almost sacred. Keep your own identity, but walk together as one. Don't ever give up on your love and marriage.

7. Settle the fact that you've made your choice and you're no longer looking for anyone else. Don't flirt. Think of the consequences. Don't consider it.

8. Be in agreement about how your money is spent. Big items should have the approval of both. Talk about how to manage your finances.

9. When in doubt about your actions, ask yourself how you would want to be treated and then act accordingly. If you've argued, never go to sleep without asking the other's forgiveness, even when you don't feel like it or want to. Be faithful about this; you won't be sorry. Do what will make you both the happiest in the long run and be the best for your marriage.

10. Have fun!

                                          ❧ Donna Fargo

Be Swift to Forgive

The purpose of forgiveness
is to unburden both our hearts
and the hearts of others
from unnecessary pain —
to free us from carrying around
   the baggage of mistakes.
In the long run, it really
   doesn't matter
who did what to whom;
what's more important
is the toll on our peace of mind
when we withhold forgiveness.
A heart full of forgiveness
   is a happy one,
and the lightness of spirit
   and good cheer
can't help but spill over
onto those around us —
and everyone wins.
So be an example.
Show the world
that the act of forgiveness
is not just letting someone
   "off the hook" —
but to heal your own spirit
and get on with life
as it was meant to be lived.

∽ Linda Hersey

Let Love Guide Your Path

There will be days when you feel
filled with love and gratitude,
happier than you ever dreamed possible.
On those days, rejoice in your love
    and be thankful for each other.
When the days come that don't feel
    quite as easy —
when you face difficulties
    and obstacles on your path —
remember to find strength in your love.
Let it be a bridge that carries you
    over the empty spaces,
that connects your hearts
    when you feel separated,
and that shows you the other side
    when you disagree.
Let love guide your path
as you walk into the future,
and every step of your journey
    will lead you to
a bright and beautiful tomorrow.

            ❧ Rachyl Taylor

A Husband and Wife Know the Greatest Love Two People Can Share

When two people fall in love and decide to get married, they make a solemn commitment to each other. They entrust each other with promises that are genuine and sincere. When these promises are realized and respected, they become a guiding light into the future.

Marriage is full of ups and downs, easy choices and difficult decisions — yet through it all, marriage prevails when love and friendship remain true. Marriage is an intricate foundation of learning. A husband and wife teach each other and learn from each other.

They share their life experiences in ways that are instrumental to personal development and spiritual growth. They can grow independently of each other to pursue their own personal endeavors while still maintaining the marital bond. This bond completes them and joins them as one, offering them dependence on each other for strength and support.

Marriage is a big step; there is no underestimating that. But when two people love each other unconditionally in the name of marriage, they can share nothing better in this world.

                          ≈ Debbie Burton-Peddle

A Marriage Wish

May your marriage be
    like a surprise package
        opened by two children.
May it be filled with wonders
    and adventures
and a treasure of shared memories
    experienced together as best friends.

May you be blessed
    with an abundance of joy.

May you always have the comfort
    of each other's loving arms
        during times of sadness.

May you learn from the past,
    enjoy the present,
and look forward to the future
    with hopeful anticipation
        of many blessings
in your journey together.

～ Debbie Avery Pirus

Marriage Is a Promise

Marriage is a covenant
   between two people
who deeply sense that their lives are,
and always will be, shared as one.

Marriage is the fulfillment of a dream
and an awareness that reality also
can bring us the beauty of dreams.

Marriage is a promise that today
is the beginning of a future
that will nurture love, respect, honor,
and mutual faith as the greatest
strengths for its foundation.

Marriage is an understanding between
two sensitive, intelligent,
   and caring people
who have evidenced that true love
can survive all obstacles and grow
stronger with the passage of time.

❧ Edith Schaffer Lederberg

The Meaning of Marriage

Marriage is the sweet
and wondrous way
two people
tell the whole world
about their love.

They say together
this is what
we've been
waiting a lifetime for.

And then... without even
having to say so much as
a single word
(except, perhaps, "I do")
they remind us all
that sometimes wishes
really can come true.

Their smiles say... with
this ring I thee wed...
while each of their hearts
whispers... we are so blessed
and all my life I am
going to cherish you...

They are what it means
to be married.
They have life's greatest
opportunity for abundance.

They can inspire
everything it takes.
And they lovingly
make the holiest
of human plans
simply by saying
about the most
valuable of all things…

"…let's share our love
and our lives together."

And all their days
in a thousand ways,
may their wishes come true
forever.

                                                   ☙ Douglas Pagels

Love Is the Most Beautiful Feeling in Marriage

Love is
the strongest feeling known
an all-encompassing passion
an extreme strength
an overwhelming excitement

Love is
trying not to hurt the other person
trying not to change
    the other person
trying not to dominate
    the other person
trying not to deceive
    the other person

Love is
understanding each other
listening to each other
supporting each other
having fun with each other

Love is
not an excuse to stop growing
not an excuse to stop
    making yourself better
not an excuse to lessen one's goals
not an excuse to take the
    other person for granted

Love is
being completely honest
    with each other
finding dreams to share
working toward common goals
sharing responsibilities equally

Everyone in the world wants to love
Love is not a feeling
    to be taken lightly
Love is a feeling to be cherished
    nurtured and cared for
Love is
the reason for life

                              Susan Polis Schutz

Remember the Vows You Made on Your Wedding Day

Marriage is not about individual differences or lifestyles, competition or anger. Marriage is a way of thinking, a way of life, that involves both of you trying your best to make each other happy.

Marriage means being proud of each other when things are going your way. It means thinking of each other's feelings even when your personal emotions are on the line. It means being thankful for the support and guidance you give each other, without comparing who gives more.

Your marriage vow means that someone hopes you are never too cold, too hot, too hungry, or too tired. It means someone thinks of you as a gift from God and cherishes every moment spent with you. It means someone wants to talk to you, be with you, and hold you in the night and tell you everything will be okay. It means someone loves you.

With this vow comes your responsibility to admire your mate's strengths, while protecting them and helping them in every way you can. It means asking for forgiveness and being thankful for the forgiveness they are willing to offer. Remember that your partner needs to be reminded throughout life that your love is unconditional. They will need to know how much you care, and will need to tell you the same.

Keep all these things in mind. The two of you were meant for each other, and you have a special gift in each other. You have the ability to share with each other and teach any glorious children you may bring into the world what it means to be truly happy.

Trust each other, support each other, listen to each other... and love each other always.

→ Jessica Avery

Together, You Can Create Miracles

Let the magic in your marriage be endless.
It will live forever if you
take the time and patience
    to make it happen.
As long as your love is nurtured
    and never taken for granted,
it will continue to grow
    into something wonderful.
Feed the fires of your passion
with tenderness, bouquets,
and moments of sweet togetherness.
Walk together through tough times
and be each other's umbrella in the storms.
Allow each other the space to grow
    and achieve.
Share many hugs, warm wishes,
    and times of hand holding,
caring, and communication.
Believe in magic, and your marriage will hold
a lifetime of love and dreams fulfilled.
May the love you feel for each other
continue to grow magically
and bring you miracles and joy.

❧ Linda C. Grazulis

In All the Days of Your Marriage...

May the highest mountains
Kneel to meet you,
And when they do not
May angels lend you their wings.
May the paths you choose
Lead you to fields of flowers
And lush green meadows,
But when you encounter barren lands
May you have the knowledge
To cultivate your own beauty.
May the harvest of your love
Always be bountiful and fulfilling,
And may you share its yield
With family and friends.
May all the days of your marriage
Be sunny ones,
But if you happen to encounter heavy storms
May they always be followed by rainbows.
Most importantly,
May your happiness shine
Brighter than the stars
And your love outlive the moon.

         Corrina Cockins

Marriage Is
a Celebration of Love

Being married is a beautiful feeling;
it makes whatever we do
seem wonderful and happy.
It gives us so many reasons
to smile,
or to tell the world
that someone is special to us —
someone who cares about us
the way we care about them.
Being married makes times of being together
go by so quickly
and times of being apart
seem to last forever.

Being married fills our lives with memories.
It is a unique feeling
that changes all the time,
but every different aspect
has a magic all its own.
The beauty of marriage is endless.
It is the essence of life
we all are longing to find,
longing to hold,
and dreaming of keeping forever
in our hearts.

                            ᴂ Deanna Beisser

Walk Through Life Hand in Hand

The union of two hearts evolves
into one, and there within it unfolds
a deeper sense of peace and gratitude
　　for what you have found.
You have explored the depths
of your love in its entirety,
and have discovered
that when your two souls touched,
　　you became whole.

You pledge to love each other,
no matter what the future holds.
You understand that pure love in its
form keeps no conditions or barriers.

It always seeks to support —
not only through times of contentment,
but also through times
of discouragement and difficulty.

May you always carry one another
throughout the passage of life,
always walking together
as you come to understand
what it means to be one.
May the sunrise that lights a new day
bring sweet joy to your hearts,
and may each new sunset leave you
with lasting memories...

But most of all, may you forever cherish
and remember the blessing of being
    husband and wife.

                                            ~ Leslie Neilson

What Is a Marriage?

It is the most beautiful thing that can happen between two people in love.

A marriage is more than just a husband and a wife. It is a bridge which allows the love of two very special people to give meaning and worth and wonder to life. It is a continual process of building; of shaping; of communicating; and caring. It is the deepest and sweetest understanding. It is sharing todays and tomorrows together and making each one more treasured and more complete than anyone could make them alone. A marriage is a home interwoven with hopes and memories and dreams. The thankfulness and love it can bring have no comparison.

Being happily married is the most beautiful thing that can happen... to anyone.

❧ Collin McCarty

The Most Wonderful Commitment in Life Is Being Married

In marriage
you make the most beautiful
commitment in life —
to love each other forever
You will share
work and play
happiness and sadness
goals and values
family and friends
excitement and boredom
You will build a life
which is stronger because
you are now part of a team —
a team which should go through life
holding hands
always cheering for each other
In marriage
you make the most beautiful
commitment in life —
two people
in love
joining together
to become
one forever

                     ❧ Susan Polis Schutz

When Two People Marry, Their Lives Are Joined in Happiness

When two people marry,
they share equally with each other.
They become one.
A bond is built, along with trust
    and loyalty.
They accept each other for what they are.
They love each other for who they are.
They are there for each other
    to comfort when they are down.
When one hurts, the other hurts.
They communicate with each other.
The problems they have are worked out.
They work on their relationship together.
They learn to grow with each other.
They accept challenges as they come.

Sometimes they are scared,
    but they are always there for one another.
They are one,
but they have their own minds,
their own ideas, and different ways
    of thinking.
They love and learn, cry and feel.
They are there to help each other.
They are not perfect; they make mistakes.
Their lives are lived happily,
when two people marry.

                        ❧ Tracey Kuharski-Miller

Two Hearts, One Love

Let your marriage be a potpourri of your love. Gather each special moment as it comes, and carefully preserve it in your heart.

Savor the good times, so that you will be strengthened when clouds hide the sun. Appreciate your togetherness, even when apart, and rejoice in your oneness. Make time for each other; it is a wise investment in your happiness.

Treasure the uniqueness of your love, for there is none other quite the same. Add the spices of laughter and dreams; they ensure a lasting quality to your love. Replenish it often with kind words and understanding hearts. And may every day become a beautiful memory.

❧ Carol R. Tanner

All You Need...
Is Each Other

Be sure to fill your marriage with roses and romance, gentle love, generous memories, and a love that celebrates your two hearts as one. Fill it with storybook tomorrows, two smiles, two sighs, one dream, and a love lived out one day at a time.

Treat each other as best friends; share your affection openly. Know in your hearts that what you share is a gift from God. Face your mountains together side by side and arm in arm. Never hold back the love you share and feel. Work as companions and enjoy each other's charms.

Remember love is for dreaming, developing, and discovering. Through life's ups and downs, never forget that your love is all you need to get you through anything.

☙ Linda E. Knight

"The Marriage Poem"

Being married is the most wonderful thing that can happen to two people in love ❧ A marriage is a caring commitment to making a miracle last forever ❧ It truthfully whispers the words "I don't know what I'd ever do without you" ❧ It joyfully says "I want you to be there in all my tomorrows" ❧ And it sings the praises of sharing life, as husband and wife, sweetly and completely together ❧ A marriage is opening the door to all the good things and best wishes around you ❧ A marriage is opening your hearts to the wonders within you ❧ A marriage is a promise to stay together, to dream together, to work on whatever needs attention, to keep love fresh and alive, and to continue to bless the beauty of your lives ❧ A marriage is reaching for the wishes you both want to come true, and remembering the priceless smiles that come from hearing "I love you" ❧

A marriage is one of life's most wondrous blessings ❧ It involves taking the words of two life stories and weaving them together on the same pages ❧ Every year, in a thousand special ways, the words that will be written in this remarkable story will reflect the strength and the joy and the love that rises above any trials and sorrows ❧ A marriage is the precious, reassuring comfort of having a kindred soul care about your day, every day and each tomorrow, your whole life long ❧

A marriage is the making of a home that seems so meant to be... between a special woman and a special man ❧ A marriage is a beautiful journey along life's road with two people
    smiling as they go,
        lovingly... hand in hand ❧

❧ Douglas Pagels

When Two People Become One...

When two people join together and bond their lives forever because they are certain they have something special that will make their marriage last... this is the first act of faith.

Upon this act of faith, these two people will build a life. And as long as their determination stays with them, this life will always be their hope, their dream, their truth, their being, their inspiration, and their source of strength.

Through their life together, they will hurt and laugh. Together, they will feel all life's ups and downs. They will learn and grow through trial and error. The lessons will show them the meaning of true love and the difference between a love that lasts and one that just gives up.

These two people will face each failure together and discover the strength to go on. They will encourage each other's dreams and forgive each other's faults.

Through a labor of love, these two will become as one — fighting against the odds and ultimately creating a marriage that will grow into an infinite love.

❦ Regina Hill

Always Remember to Say "I Love You"

Too many times it seems we take for granted the ones we love. We wait for birthdays or holidays or some other special occasion to say "I love you," "I appreciate you," or "thank you." We let life carry us away on a never-ending road filled with the responsibilities of a day-to-day existence.

In our busy lives, we often forget that there is more along the way than just bills to pay, phone calls to return, and errands to run. There are people in our lives who need to be hugged, who need to be loved. There are people in our lives who need their accomplishments noticed and praised. We need to remember how fragile hearts can be, how quickly a soul can grow weary, how fast a spirit can break...

A heart is like a garden that needs to be tended to and nourished with what only another heart can give — love and appreciation, devotion and honesty.

∞ Tracia Gloudemans

Marriage Is a Lifetime Journey of Love

Marriage is a journey. There are no maps. There is only a commitment to stay on the same path — to love, honor, and cherish each other every day.

Always be truthful. Respect the fact that you are different people with individual needs and wants. Support and encourage each other's dreams. Be yourselves. Keep your word. Be there for each other when the world outside threatens to knock you down. Hold each other up. Stand up for your love. Be true to yourselves, even if other people don't like your truth.

Remember the little things. Actions may speak louder than words, but when someone looks you in the eye, takes you in their arms, and says "I love you," nothing else matters. Understand that even anger is a form of communication, but it puts up walls and wastes time where happiness could have been.

Say "I'm sorry." Forgiveness can make your love grow stronger. Say what you mean; mean what you say. Be gentle; cry together.

Flowers are nice once in a while; so is a night out with the boys. Talk a lot to each other; listen even more. Don't expect perfection, only effort. Learn from your mistakes. Remember that laughter heals, so laugh a lot together. Admit when you're wrong or you just don't know something. Be responsible for the happiness you bring into your own life; don't expect your partner to fulfill all your needs.

Marriage is not a guarantee of anything... but the space surrounded by your love should always be a safe place to fall, a sanctuary and home where love endures. Marriage is a journey, not a destination. Travel far together, for many years. Don't take for granted each other or all the special moments along the way. Love gently, and always remember you hold each other's heart.

  Cindy VanDenBosch

ACKNOWLEDGMENTS

We gratefully acknowledge the permission granted by the following authors, publishers, and authors' representatives to reprint poems or excerpts from their publications.

Jacqueline Schiff for "If You Want to Share the Best Kind of Love...." Copyright © 2004 by Jacqueline Schiff. All rights reserved.

Linda E. Knight for "Cherish Your Anniversary" and "All You Need... Is Each Other." Copyright © 2004 by Linda E. Knight. All rights reserved.

PrimaDonna Entertainment Corp. for "10 Ways to Have a Happy Marriage" and "Anniversaries Are for Remembering..." by Donna Fargo. Copyright © 2000, 2004 by PrimaDonna Entertainment Corp. All rights reserved.

Barbara Cage for "A Dozen Rules for Couples to Live By." Copyright © 2004 by Barbara Cage. All rights reserved.

Carol Howard for "Let There Be No Limits to Your Love." Copyright © 2004 by Carol Howard. All rights reserved.

Linda Hersey for "Be Swift to Forgive." Copyright © 2004 by Linda Hersey. All rights reserved.

Debbie Burton-Peddle for "A Husband and Wife Know the Greatest Love Two People Can Share." Copyright © 2004 by Debbie Burton-Peddle. All rights reserved.

Debbie Avery Pirus for "A Marriage Wish." Copyright © 2004 by Debbie Avery Pirus. All rights reserved.

Edith Schaffer Lederberg for "Marriage Is a Promise." Copyright © 1990 by Edith Schaffer Lederberg. All rights reserved.

Jessica Avery for "Remember the Vows You Made on Your Wedding Day." Copyright © 2004 by Jessica Avery. All rights reserved.

Linda C. Grazulis for "Together, You Can Create Miracles." Copyright © 2004 by Linda C. Grazulis. All rights reserved.

Corrina Cockins for "In All the Days of Your Marriage...." Copyright © 2004 by Corrina Cockins. All rights reserved.

Deanna Beisser for "Marriage Is a Celebration of Love." Copyright © 1990 by Deanna Beisser. All rights reserved.

Leslie Neilson for "Walk Through Life Hand in Hand." Copyright © 2004 by Leslie Neilson. All rights reserved.

Carol R. Tanner for "Two Hearts, One Love." Copyright © 2004 by Carol R. Tanner. All rights reserved.

Cindy VanDenBosch for "Marriage Is a Lifetime Journey of Love." Copyright © 2004 by Cindy VanDenBosch. All rights reserved.

A careful effort has been made to trace the ownership of selections used in this anthology in order to obtain permission to reprint copyrighted material and give proper credit to the copyright owners. If any error or omission has occurred, it is completely inadvertent, and we would like to make corrections in future editions provided that written notification is made to the publisher:

BLUE MOUNTAIN ARTS, INC., P.O. Box 4549, Boulder, Colorado 80306.